ReCAP Workbo

To Kill a Mockingbird

by Harper Lee

SCHOOLHOUSE

Designing literature-based learning experience

To Kill a Mockingbird

ReCAP Workbook

Copyright ©2022 Schoolhouse LLC

All rights reserved.

Copyrighted Material

Published by SCHOOLHOUSE LLC

Centreville, VA 20120

Contact@schoolhouseacademy.org

About Schoolhouse and ReCAP

Schoolhouse began as a small tutoring service with a strong belief that books and literary works contain some of the most valuable lessons for the growth of the mind. Through years of trial and error with numerous students, we've connected the joy of reading with structured English language learning: a set of tailored questions on reading comprehension, vocabulary and literary techniques, and critical and analytical thinking, all inspired directly by the plot, characters, and literary devices from the book.

We call this educational method the ReCAP method (Reading Comprehension & Analysis Program). This book is a result of our work to further standardize the ReCAP method, in order to make it accessible to the broader group of students, parents, teachers, and any individuals in the education scene to provide a flexible, engaging, and meaningful learning experience.

Every chapter has a corresponding set of ReCAP questions arranged in the order of the progression of the plot in the story. You will find that these questions hone in on specific aspects of the plot, interactions and relationships between different characters, the author's intentions, and other important elements from the book. Naturally, they require a basic understanding of the story, but also call for a variety of English language skills including but not limited to character analysis, making inferences, parts of speech, figurative language, and diction.

Our mission has been, and will always be, to design engaging and meaningful learning experiences that will improve the English language skills for students in grades K – 12.

Table of contents

⟫⟫ Pre-reading Discussion

There are situations where people might think you've done something bad, even though you haven't done anything.

If you were innocent, would you run away from such situations that might get you in trouble? Why or why not?

>>> Characters in the Story

Jean Louise Finch (Scout): the main character

Jeremy Atticus Finch (Jem): Scout's older brother

Atticus Finch: Scout's father, a lawyer in Maycomb County

John Hale Finch (Uncle Jack): Atticus's younger brother, a doctor

Alexandra Finch (Aunt): Atticus's younger sister

Calpurnia: The Finches' cook

Arthur Radley (Boo Radley): a neighbor; a recluse

Nathan Radley: Boo Radley's older brother

Mrs. Radley: Arthur and Nathan Radley's mother

Charles Baker Harris (Dill): Miss Rachel's nephew, a boy from Mississippi

Miss Rachel: Dill's aunt, a neighbor

Miss Maudie Atkinson: a neighbor

Mrs. Henry Lafayette Dubose: a neighbor

Miss Stephanie Crawford: a neighbor

Reverend Sykes: Reverend of the First Purchase, a colored church

Mr. Dolphus Raymond: a man who is believed to be drunk

Tom Robinson: the defendant

Robert Ewell (Bob Ewell): a mean, alcoholic and ignorant man; Mayella's father; the witness in Tom Robinson's trial

Mayella Violet Ewell: the witness in Tom Robinson's trial, Tom Robinson's accuser

Mr. Heck Tate: the witness in Tom Robinson's trial, the sheriff of Maycomb County

Mr. Gilmer: the prosecuting attorney

(Mr. Atticus Finch: the defense attorney)

Judge Taylor: The judge in Tom Robinson's trial

Mr. B. B. Underwood: The owner, writer and editor of the Maycomb Tribune

》》 Pre-reading Activity

▷ Vocabulary List

1)	Aberration	straying from the right or normal way
2)	Accost	approach to speak
3)	Acquittal	discharge of an offence
4)	Acrimonious	bitter; caustic; acerbic
5)	Adamant	resolute; unyielding
6)	Adjacent	nearby; adjoining something else
7)	Affirmative	assenting; approving; agreeing with
8)	Ambidextrous	able to use both hands equally well
9)	Antagonize	cause to become hostile; oppose
10)	Apoplectic	extremely indignant
11)	Arbitrate	reach a settlement; determine
12)	Articulate	say clearly; express coherently
13)	Ascertain	make certain; make sure of
14)	Assuage	soothe; alleviate
15)	Attentive	paying attention to; concentrating
16)	Auspicious	favorable; being a good omen
17)	Bestow	bequeath; confer; grant

18) Candid — honest; straightforward; truthful

19) Chronic — constantly recurring; long-lasting

20) Concede — accept; relinquish; admit

21) Condescend — show feelings of superiority

22) Congregation — assembled group for religious worship

23) Connivance — consent to wrongdoing; conspiracy

24) Contemptuous — arrogant; scornful

25) Contraband — goods imported or exported illegally

26) Contradict — belie; deny the truth of

27) Cordial — friendly; amicable

28) Corroborate — authenticate; substantiate

29) Countenance — appearance of the face; visage

30) Decree — order rule; declare

31) Degeneration — decline; deterioration

32) Demur — disagree; show reluctance

33) Deportation — banishment; expulsion

34) Devout — sincerely believing; faithful

35) Discreet — prudent; careful in one's actions

36) Disorderly — undisciplined; disorganized

37) Dispel — drive away thought; eliminate

38) Disposition	personal temperament; propensity
39) Domicile	residence; dwelling
40) Ecclesiastical	relating to the Christian Church
41) Edification	improvement; education
42) Ensue	happen as a result
43) Entailment	ramification; repercussion; consequence
44) Enunciate	articulate; pronounce clearly
45) Façade	exterior of a building; front
46) Fluctuation	vacillation; inconstancy
47) Frivolous	trivial; not having any value
48) Gravitate	be drawn toward; incline
49) Guileless	innocent; without deception
50) Illiterate	unable to read and write; ignorant
51) Immaterial	irrelevant; meaningless; unimportant
52) Impassive	aloof; stolid; stoic
53) Impediment	obstruction in doing something; hindrance
54) Inconsistent	contradictory; not in keeping with
55) Inconspicuous	not clearly visible; unnoticeable
56) Indigenous	aboriginal; endemic; native
57) Indulge	satiate; entertain oneself

58) Iniquity   immoral behavior; corruption; depravity

59) Inquisitive   curious; inquiring

60) Invective   verbal abuse; abusive language

61) Invoke   call upon; appeal to

62) Judicious   having good judgment; thoughtful

63) Literate   able to read and write; educated

64) Martyr   sufferer; saint

65) Meditative   contemplative; introspective

66) Mortification   great embarrassment and shame

67) Obstreperous   boisterous; difficult to control

68) Obtrusive   noticeable in an intrusive way; projecting

69) Ominous   portentous; apocalyptic; menacing

70) Overture   introduction; approach; proposition

71) Perpetrate   carry out; execute; commit

72) Perpetual   constant; never changing

73) Persecution   ill-treatment; affliction; harassment

74) Placid   calm; not easily upset

75) Prejudiced   biased; bigoted; one-sided

76) Prominent   outstanding; conspicuous; noticeable

77) Prosecute   bring action against; execute; carry off

78) Quell   put an end to; subdue; suppress

79) Reminiscent   provoking a memory; recollective

80) Reprimand   admonish; rebuke; chide

81) Reverent   showing respect; deferential

82) Rueful   regretful; mournful

83) Scrutiny   close examination; critical observation

84) Speculation   conjecture without evidence; thought

85) Spurious   inauthentic; false; counterfeit

86) Strenuous   requiring great exertion; arduous

87) Succinct   terse; to the point; concise

88) Taciturn   uncommunicative; laconic

89) Temerity   audacity; excessive boldness

90) Tenet   principle; belief; doctrine

91) Testify   give testimony; give evidence as a witness

92) Truant   absent; no-show; missing

93) Unanimous   in agreement; united

94) Uncompromising   not allowing for any exceptions; stubborn

95) Unmitigated   absolute; unqualified; complete

96) Vapid   lacking liveliness; not stimulating

97) Vehement   showing strong aggressiveness; fierce

98) Venerable   respected; revered

▷ Sentence Making

Make your own sentences using the following words.

1. acquit

_____

_____

_____

2. contradict

_____

_____

_____

3. disorderly

_____

_____

_____

4. dispel

_____

_____

5. inquisitive

6. mortify

7. prejudiced

8. speculate

9. testify

10. unanimous

11. uncompromising

12. vehement

⟫ After-reading Discussion

▷ Short Answer Questions

Part One

<Chapter 1~4>

1) In Chapter 1, why does Scout say, "the battles between Calpurnia and her are one-sided"?

_____

_____

_____

2) In Chapter 1, when Jem, Scout and Dill feel bored of repeating the same activities, what new idea does Dill come up with?

_____

_____

_____

3) In Chapter 1, what makes Jem run through the gate and touch the Radley House?

_____

_____

_____

4) In Chapter 2, how does Scout's teacher, Miss Caroline, react to Scout's literacy?

_____

_____

_____

5) In Chapter 2, why doesn't Walter Cunningham Jr. bring his lunch to school?

_____

_____

_____

6) In Chapter 3, why does Jem invite Walter Cunningham Jr. to dinner after the fight?

_____

_____

_____

7) In Chapter 3, why does Calpurnia make cracking bread on Scout's first day of school?

_____

_____

_____

8) In Chapter 3, why does Scout tell Atticus that she doesn't want to go to school anymore?

_____

_____

9) In Chapter 3, according to Atticus, what is a compromise? Which school policy do Atticus and Scout compromise on?

10) In Chapter 4, what does Scout find in the knot-hole in the oak tree at the edge of the Radley Place?

11) In Chapter 4, what do Jem and Scout think is the most exciting part of the summer?

12) According to Jem in Chapter 4, what will the two Indian head pennies bring to him?

<Chapter 5~8>

13) In Chapter 5, why do Jem and Dill want to write a note to Boo Radley?

_____

_____

_____

14) In Chapter 5, Atticus sees Jem trying to put something on the window sill of the Radley House for Boo Radley. When Atticus asks Jem what he has been doing, why does Jem say he was putting a letter for Mr. Nathan Radley?

_____

_____

_____

15) In Chapter 6, Jem, Scout and Dill run away from the Radley House after they try to peek into the house through one of the windows. When Atticus asks Jem why he is not wearing his pants, what excuse does Dill improvise?

_____

_____

_____

16) Jem and Scout find some interesting objects in the knot-hole in the oak tree at the Radley House. How do they decide if something they find isn't someone else's property?

_____

_____

17) In Chapter 7, Jem and Scout find two soap figurines in the knot-hole in the oak tree. What do they assume the figurines represent?

18) When Jem and Scout are thinking about writing a thank-you letter to the person who has been leaving presents in the knot-hole, what do they find has happened to the knot-hole?

19) In Chapter 8, a small amount of snowfall happens overnight, for the first time since 1885. What brilliant idea does Jem have to make a snowman with the insufficient amount of snow? Why does Jem's idea impress Atticus?

20) On the night Jem and Scout make a snowman, what disastrous event happens to Miss Maudie's house?

21) In Chapter 8, Scout finds herself wrapped with a brown blanket after watching the fire. How does she get the blanket?

<Chapter 9~11>

22) In Chapter 9, regarding Atticus's defense of Tom Robinson, what does Atticus ask Scout to do for him?

23) In Chapter 9, Atticus, Jem and Scout visit Aunt Alexandra's house, the Landing, for Christmas. Why is Aunt Alexandra "fanatical" about Scout's attire?

24) In the beginning of Chapter 10, why does Scout feel ashamed of Atticus? And later in this chapter, what makes Scout proud of Atticus?

25) In Chapter 11, why does Jem ruin Mrs. Dubose's camellia bush?

26) In Chapter 11, when Jem goes to Mrs. Dubose to apologize, what does Mrs. Dubose ask Jem to do for her?

Part Two

<Chapter 12~15>

27) In Chapter 12, what makes Calpurnia consider taking Jem and Scout to her church, the First Purchase, the next day?

28) In Chapter 12, what makes Jem think that some people at Calpurnia's church don't want him and Scout to worship in their church?

29) In Chapter 13, why does the author remark that the people in Maycomb look faintly alike?

30) In Chapter 14, why has Dill run away from home?

31) In Chapter 15, Atticus leaves home after dinner one night. Out of curiosity, Jem, Scout and Dill follow after him. Where do they find Atticus in the middle of the night, and what is Atticus doing?

<Chapter 16~19>

32) In Chapter 16, Aunt Alexandra tells Atticus that talking about other people in front of Calpurnia is not a good habit. What does Aunt Alexandra think Calpurnia can do when Calpurnia overhears their conversation?

33) In Chapter 16, according to Atticus, how did Jem and Scout's presence on the previous night affect Mr. Walter Cunningham?

34) In Chapter 17, after Mr. Ewell's testimony, why does Atticus repeatedly ask Mr. Ewell if he asked for a doctor for his daughter?

35) In Chapter 17, after Atticus has confirmed that Mayella is beaten on her right eye, why does he ask Mr. Ewell if he is literate and can write his name?

36) When Atticus has proved that Mayella got injured on the right side of her body, and Mr. Ewell is left-handed, why does Scout think these are not enough evidence to determine Mr. Ewell as the assailant?

37) In the beginning of Chapter 18, why does Mayella Ewell think that Atticus is mortifying her?

38) In Chapter 18, what is Atticus's intention behind asking Tom Robinson to stand up in front of the judge?

39) In Chapter 19, why does Scout think Mayella Ewell may be lonelier than Boo Radley?

40) In Chapter 19, according to Tom Robinson, why has he been helping Mayella without any compensation?

41) In Chapter 19, what is the reason Dill starts crying during the trial?

42) In Chapter 19, why is Mr. Link Deas, Tom Robinson's employer of eight years, told to leave the court?

<Chapter 20~23>

43) In the beginning of Chapter 20, what truth about Mr. Dolphus Raymond's drinking habit do Scout and Dill find out?

---

44) In Chapter 21, why does Aunt Alexandra send Calpurnia to the courtroom?

---

45) In Chapter 21, why does Reverend Sykes say that he is not so confident about the verdict even though it is clear that Judge Taylor is leaning to Tom Robinson's side?

---

46) In Chapter 22, who brings all kinds of food for Atticus in the next morning of Tom Robinson's trial, and why?

---

47) In Chapter 22, what encouraging remarks does Miss Maudie make to Jem and Scout regarding keeping a jury out for so long in a case involving a black man?

48) In Chapter 23, Atticus says that there is a Cunningham on the jury in Tom Robinson's trial. What about Cunningham's behavior does Atticus find to be significant?

<Chapter 24~27>

49) In Chapter 24, why does Atticus come home earlier than his usual time?

50) In Chapter 25, how does Dill describe Helen Robinson's reaction to her husband's death?

51) In Chapter 26, what do you think Mr. Ewell meant when he reportedly said, "one down and about two more to go"? Why do you think so?

52) In Chapter 27, according to Scout, what are the three notable events that have happened by the middle of October in Maycomb?

\<Chapter 28~31\>

53) On their way home after the Halloween pageant, why are Jem and Scout alarmed?

54) In Chapter 28, what items that belong to Scout does Mr. Tate find at the crime scene?

55) In the beginning of Chapter 29, why does Aunt Alexandra say she is responsible for Bob's attacking Jem and Scout?

56) In Chapter 29, according to Mr. Tate, what saved Scout's life from Bob's attack?

57) In Chapter 31, Scout takes Boo Radley home after the gathering at the Finches. As Scout recollects the series of events for the past two years, what makes her feel sad?

58) In Chapter 31, how does Scout practice Atticus's words, "You never really know a man until you stand in his shoes and walk around in them."?

▷ In-depth Writing Questions

Answer each question in complete sentences. You may find clues to your answer in the book.

Part One

<Chapter 1~4>

1) Describe Atticus as a father. How does Atticus discipline his children?

_____

_____

_____

_____

_____

_____

_____

2) In Chapter 2, why do you think Scout's first grade teacher, Miss Caroline, fails to establish her authority in the classroom? Provide your reasoning.

3) In Chapter 3, Scout tells Atticus about her teacher and the happenings on the first day of school. According to Atticus, how should the students try to view their teacher's behavior to better understand it?

4) In Chapter 4, what are the two reasons Scout wants to quit the Boo Radley game?

<Chapter 5~8>

5) In Chapter 6, what makes Mr. Nathan Radley shoot his gun? If you were Jem or Scout, how would you explain to Atticus how you entered the Radleys' property and lost Jem's pants?

In Chapter 7, after school starts, Jem tells Scout that he found his pants on the Radley's fence neatly mended and folded when he went to retrieve them on the day after the incident. Why do you think Jem didn't tell Scout about it earlier?

6) Discuss Miss Maudie's reaction to the fire of the previous night that completely burned down her house and her garden. Give three examples that show her attitude.

<Chapter 9~11>

7) In the beginning of Chapter 10, Atticus says, "It's a sin to kill a mockingbird." According to Miss Maudie's comment on Atticus's statement, why is killing a mockingbird a sin?

If "a mockingbird" were to be referring to Boo Radley, what would "killing" mean?

8) In Chapter 11, Atticus makes Jem apologize to Mrs. Dubose for having ruined her garden. What was the reason Jem ruined her garden? Considering the reason behind Jem's action, do you think it is reasonable for Jem to apologize to Mrs. Dubose? Why or why not?

9) In Chapter 11, why does Atticus agree to defend Tom Robinson, a black man who is accused of raping a white woman, even though he has more to lose than to gain from the case?

Do you think defending Tom Robinson for justice will help him earn fame and respect in the long run? Why or why not?

Part Two

<Chapter 12~15>

10) In Chapter 14, Atticus and Aunt Alexandra get into an argument about Calpurnia taking Jem and Scout to her church in the black community. What different perspectives do Atticus and Aunt Alexandra have about Calpurnia's conduct? Why does Jem say that he and Scout should not antagonize Aunt Alexandra?

<Chapter 16~19>

11) In Chapter 16, Mr. Dolphus Raymond is known to be drinking whiskey all the time, and sitting with colored people. What difficult situation

causes Mr. Raymond to be drunk? What makes him prefer to associate with black people, rather than white people?

12) Discuss Tom Robinson's case by answering each of the following questions.

What crime is Tom accused of committing?

What is particularly strange and incomprehensible in Mr. Bob Ewell's handling of the situation when he finds her daughter raped and cruelly beaten?

What is the most compelling evidence that supports Tom Robinson's innocence?

13) Compare and contrast Mr. Bob Ewell and Mr. Dolphus Raymond by their social status, living conditions and values.

14) In Chapter 19, Tom Robinson says that he ran away from the Ewell's place because he was scared. Why would he be scared when he didn't do any harm to Mayella?

Do you think Tom Robinson would have taken the same action if he was white? Share your thoughts.

15) Based on your response to Question 14, discuss the racial prejudice that openly pervaded white community in the Southern states of America in the 1930s. Provide some examples.

<Chapter 20~23>

16) In Chapter 20, what is Mayella Ewell guilty of doing?

What is Mr. Bob Ewell guilty of doing?

17) In Chapter 20, according to Atticus, what "cynical confidence" do Bob
and Mayella have in giving their testimony?

What does Atticus mean when he describes their confidence to be based
on "the evil assumption"?

18) Atticus is going to appeal to a higher court against the court decision. What do you think will happen when the higher court reviews Tom Robinson's case? Choose one of the following scenarios and provide your reasoning for your choice.

    a. Tom Robinson will be acquitted after the court's review.

    b. The higher court will turn down the appeal.

    c. There will be a new trial, and Tom Robinson will win.

    d. There will be a new trial, and Tom Robinson will lose.

....

....

....

....

....

....

....

19) In Chapter 23, Atticus says that it is the shadow of a beginning that it took a few hours for the jury to give a final guilty verdict in the trial. Why is it "the shadow of a beginning"? Explain.

<Chapter 24~27>

20) In the beginning of Chapter 25, Scout tries to kill a roly-poly, a small bug, but Jem stops her. What does Jem say when Scout asks why she can't kill the bug?

And later in this chapter, Mr. B. B. Underwood writes an editorial on Tom Robinson's death in the Maycomb Tribune. What comparison does Mr. Underwood make to mourn Tom's death?

How does that comparison help explain the title of the book?

21) In Chapter 26, Scout's teacher, Miss Gates, explains the difference between America and Germany of that time (1933~1935). What are the historical backgrounds of the two countries and why does she compare them?

Miss Gates maintains that it is not right to persecute anybody under any circumstances. According to Scout, how does Miss Gates contradict herself when it comes to the issue of black people?

<Chapter 28~31>

22) In Chapter 29, how does Scout describe her first impression of Mr. Arthur Radley? How is Arthur's appearance different from "Boo Radley" in her imagination in the beginning of the book?

23) Through the Chapters 29, 30 and 31, what about Scout's statements indicate that she is not afraid of ,or hostile to, Mr. Arthur Radley? Provide some examples.

24) In Chapter 30, Mr. Tate and Atticus have an argument on how Bob Ewell died. What are their views, and why is Atticus reluctant to agree with Mr. Tate?

At the end of the argument, what convinces Atticus to agree with Mr. Tate?

》》》 After-reading Assessment

▷ Literary Analysis: Multiple-choice Questions

Part One

\<Chapter 1~4\>

1) According to Scout, which of the following is true about Maycomb County?

    a. Maycomb County is an old, sweltering-hot place.
    b. Maycomb County is the most poverty-stricken place in Alabama.
    c. Maycomb County is the most unprejudiced place in Alabama.
    d. Maycomb County has employed an integrated school system.

2) When Jem and Scout were young, why was their summertime boundary limited from Mrs. Dubose's house to the Radley House?

    a. It was the safest area in the county.
    b. It was within calling distance of Calpurnia.
    c. Atticus allowed them to play within that boundary.
    d. Jem and Scout never had been beyond that boundary.

3) In Chapter 1, who is the "malevolent phantom"?

    a. Mr. Radley

    b. Mrs. Radley

    c. Nathan Radley

    d. Arthur Radley

4) Which of the following is <u>not</u> considered as a "Maycomb's way"?

    a. going to church to worship on Sundays

    b. Closing the shutters and doors on Sundays

    c. Having mid-morning coffee break with neighbors

    d. Joining a missionary circle

5) In Chapter 2, who has been teaching Scout to write?

    a. Boo Radley

    b. Calpurnia

    c. Jem Finch

    d. Miss Caroline

6) In Chapter 3 which of the following is most likely to be a lesson Miss Caroline learned from the first day of school?

    a. Never try to teach her students manners.

    b. Never let the Finches teach themselves.

    c. Never hand something to a Cunningham.

    d. Never mention the Dewey Decimal System.

7) In Chapter 4, what different game does Jem want to play with Dill and Scout?

    a. Pretend Calpurnia

    b. Pretend Atticus

    c. Pretend Aunt Alexandra

    d. Pretend Boo Radley

\<Chapter 5~8\>

8) In Chapter 5, what do Jem, Dill and Scout use to give a note to Boo Radley?

    a. A fishing pole

    b. A branch of an oak tree

    c. Atticus's cane

    d. A broomstick

9) In Chapter 6, which of the following activities do Jem, Scout and Dill do on Dill's last night in Maycomb?

    a. They go to Atticus's office to get permission to travel with Dill.

    b. They enter the backyard of the Radley house to see a glimpse of Boo Radley.

c. They draw an imaginary picture of Boo Radley to make fun of him.

d. They make a statue of Mr. Avery to show it to Atticus.

10) Which of the following is a personification?

a. I tried to climb into his skin and walk around in it.

b. The shadow was as crisp as toast.

c. Their porch was bathed in moonlight.

d. I smell a ghost in this house.

11) In Chapter 7, who has filled up the knot-hole in the oak tree with cement, and why?

a. Mr. Nathan Radley has filled up the hole because he found out that the tree was dying.

b. Boo Radley has filled up the hole because he runs out of gifts.

c. Atticus has filled up the hole because he doesn't like his kids to get items from unknown sources.

d. Calpurnia has filled up the hole because Jem and Scout don't come straight home from school.

12) In Chapter 8, what makes Scout think the world is ending?

a. Thunder

b. Lightening

c. Tornado

d. Snow

13) In Chapter 8, Jem and Scout think their snowman resembles:

a. Miss Maudie

b. Dill

c. Mr. Avery

d. Calpurnia

14) In Chapter 8, what makes their snowman, "Absolute Morphodite," go black and crumble?

a. Water from a fire hose

b. Heavy rain

c. The big fire

d. Hot and humid weather

<Chapter 9~11>

15) In Chapter 9, Scout overhears Atticus tell Uncle Jack about Tom Robinson's case that he has been appointed to. What can you infer from the conversation?

a. Most of the people in Maycomb will take Tom Robinson's side against Mr. Ewell's.

b. Atticus and Uncle Jack are sure that Tom Robinson's trial is going to be postponed.

c. Most of the white people in Maycomb will take Mr. Ewell's word against Tom Robinson's.

d. Aunt Alexandra is going to visit them to watch Atticus defend Tom Robinson.

16) In Chapter 10, Atticus says, "It's a _____ to kill a mockingbird." Which of the following is the word he used?

a. crime

b. sin

c. pleasure

d. sport

17) In Chapter 10, what happens to Mr. Harry's dog, Tom Johnson?

a. Tom Johnson gets poisoned.

b. Tom Johnson gets lost in the street.

c. Tom Johnson kills someone else's dog.

d. Tom Johnson gets infected by rabies.

18) In Chapter 10, according to Miss Maudie, who had a nickname, "Ol' One-Shot," when he was a boy?

a. Atticus Finch

b. Miss Maudie's husband

c. Uncle Jack

d. Mr. Heck Tate

19) In Chapter 11, why does Mrs. Dubose call Atticus before she passes away?

a. To write her will

b. To give Jem a camellia in a candy box

c. To write her will and give Jem a camellia in a candy box

d. None of the above

20) Which of the following is a metaphor?

a. My dress came up like a tent when I sat down.

b. Summer was Dill by the fishpool.

c. Smoke was rolling off the house like fog off a river bank.

d. Her hand was as wide as a bed slat.

Part Two

<Chapter 12~15>

21) In Chapter 12, why does Reverend Sykes, the preacher of the First Purchase, say their offering of that Sunday needs to reach ten dollars?

    a. They are going to help Tom Robinson survive in the jail.

    b. They are going to help Helen survive with her children.

    c. They are going to purchase goods to help the Ewells.

    d. They are going to help prisoners in the Maycomb jail.

22) In Chapter 13, Atticus tells Jem and Scout that they should try to live up to their name, Finch. Which of the following is <u>not</u> "living up to their name"?

    a. Jem must behave like the gentleman.

    b. Scout must behave like the little lady.

    c. Jem must behave like Atticus.

    d. Scout must behave like Jem.

23) In Chapter 14, Scout steps on something warm, smooth and alive in her bedroom. What does she think it is?

    a. A snake

    b. A frog

c. A puppy

d. A kitten

24) In Chapter 15, according to the author, which of the following is not true about the Maycomb jail?

    a. The jail is the most venerable building in the county.

    b. The jail is built in Gothic style like other neighboring stores.

    c. The jail is the most hideous building in the county.

    d. The jail is completely out of place in the town.

25) In Chapter 15, which acquaintance does Scout spot among the mob in front of the Maycomb jail?

    a. Mr. Heck Tate

    b. Reverend Sykes

    c. Tom Robinson

    d. Mr. Walter Cunningham

<Chapter 16~19>

26) In Chapter 16, people from various places gather in the Maycomb County courthouse to watch Tom Robinson's trial. From where do Jem, Scout and Dill watch the trial?

    a. From the colored balcony

    b. From the next row of Tom Robinson

    c. From the space behind the curtain

    d. From the next row of Mayella Ewell

27) In Chapter 17, how does the author describe the Ewells' living conditions?

    a. Hygienic and spacious

    b. Unpolluted and unwholesome

    c. Impoverished and unsanitary

    d. Contaminated and salubrious

28) In Chapter 17, how does Atticus prove that Mr. Ewell is left-handed?

    a. Atticus asks Mr. Ewell if he can write his name with his right hand.

    b. Atticus shows Judge Taylor a letter with Mr. Ewell's signature.

    c. Atticus convinces Mayella Ewell to confess that her father is left-handed.

    d. Atticus asks Mr. Ewell to write his name in front of the judge.

29) In Chapter 18, which of the following is <u>not</u> true?

    a. All people at the courthouse pay close attention to the testimonies.

    b. Atticus tries to begin with general questions, then narrows down to specific questions.

    c. Mayella's testimonies indicate to the audience that she has never been treated with respect.

    d. All of the four witnesses tell the truth to respect the oath.

30) In Chapter 18 and 19, comparing Tom's version of the event with that of Mayella's, which of the following statements is true?

    a. Tom Robinson testifies that he has been inside Mayella's fence several times to help her do chores, but Mayella testifies that she has never invited Tom inside her fence except for the day of the incident.

    b. Tom Robinson testifies that he has known Mayella since he frequently passes by the Ewell place, but Mayella says that she hasn't been acquainted with Tom until the day of the incident.

    c. Tom Robinson testifies that he has been helping Mayella from time to time for no compensation, but Mayella says that she has paid a nickel whenever Tom helps her.

   d.   Tom Robinson testifies that Mayella grabbed him first while he was helping her with the chiffarobe, but Mayella says that she was just trying to help him do the work.

31) In Chapter 19, after hearing Tom Robinson's testimony, Scout thinks Tom Robinson's manners resemble:

   a.   Those of Calpurnia's
   b.   Those of Atticus's
   c.   Those of Dill's
   d.   Those of Bob's

<Chapter 20~23>

32) In Chapter 20, according to Mr. Dolphus Raymond, why does he pretend to be drunk?

   a.   He wants to avoid tax and other responsibilities as a landowner.
   b.   He wants to show people that he is ignorant and nonchalant about the trial.
   c.   He tries to make people believe that he is too drunk to change his ways.

d. He needs more time to decide which side he should be while pretending to be drunk.

33) In Chapter 20, according to Atticus, who savagely beat Mayella Ewell?

a. Mr. Bob Ewell

b. Tom Robinson

c. Arthur Radley

d. Mr. Heck Tate

34) In Chapter 20, why does Atticus mention Thomas Jefferson in his closing statement?

a. To edify people at the courthouse that Thomas Jefferson was one of the founding fathers in the United States.

b. To emphasize that Thomas Jefferson's phrase, "All men are created equal," is supposed to be practiced in courts.

c. To propose an exception to Thomas Jefferson's phrase, "All men are created equal."

d. To demonstrate that Thomas Jefferson's phrase, "All men are created equal," has been applied to the verdict.

35) In Chapter 21, Tom Robinson is declared _____ by the verdict of the jury.

a. Innocent

b. Undecided

c. Guilty

d. Unanimous

36) In Chapter 23, who attacks Atticus on the corner of the post office?

a. Tom Robinson

b. Mr. Heck Tate

c. Mayella Ewell

d. Mr. Bob Ewell

37) Which of the following statements is true in most of the trials in Alabama in the 1930s?

a. Judges have the power to fix the penalty in capital cases.

b. A white man always wins if it was against a black man.

c. Rape is not considered as a capital offense in Alabama.

d. A jury's vote is supposed to be open to the public in Alabama.

38) What happens if a jury gives a verdict of not guilty?

a. The defendant appeals to a higher court.

b. The defendant gets acquitted.

c. The defendant gets sentenced to death.

d. The defendant confesses his/her crime.

\<Chapter 24~27\>

39) In Chapter 24, which of the following distinctly contrasts with the news of Tom Robinson's death?

a. Miss Maudie's silent consolation

b. Aunt Alexandra's shaking voice

c. Calpurnia's mourning

d. The missionary ladies' marry chatting

40) "Miss Stephanie is an English Channel of gossip."

In this quote from Chapter 25, which of the following figurative languages is used?

a. Personification

b. Metaphor

c. Simile

d. Symbolism

41) "… but in <u>the secret courts of men's hearts</u>, Atticus had no case."

In this quote from Chapter 25, what can the underlined phrase best be replaced with?

    a. The secret courts

    b. Men's consciousness

    c. Men's conscience

    d. The secret meetings

42) What do the items, the two Indian-head pennies, soap dolls, and a broken watch and chain, have in common?

    a. They are the items Dill has brought from his hometown.

    b. They are the items Jem and Scout have found in the knot-hole.

    c. They are the items Calpurnia allows Jem and Scout to play with.

    d. They are the items Atticus has bought for Jem and Scout.

43) In the beginning of Chapter 26, which of the following is <u>not</u> true about Scout's recollection of the Radley Place?

    a. Scout feels remorseful about her pranks to make Boo Radley come out.

b. Even though not any more terrified, Scout still feels the Radley Place chilly and uninviting.

c. Even though Scout is not interested in Boo Radley any more, she still wants to visit the Radleys someday.

d. Scout cannot forget the good memories about the knot-hole in the oak tree.

44) In Chapter 27, according to Atticus, why might Bob Ewell have broken into Judge Taylor's house?

a. Bob Ewell felt humiliated by Judge Taylor at Tom Robinson's trial.

b. Judge Taylor didn't render Tom Robinson a judgment of conviction.

c. Judge Taylor implied that Tom Robinson would soon be acquitted.

d. Bob Ewell was not given enough time to give his testimony at Tom Robinson's trial.

45) In Chapter 27, what food role is Scout assigned to dress up as, at the Halloween pageant?

a. Butter bean

b. Ham

c. Cow

d. Peanut

<Chapter 28~31>

46) In Chapter 28, how do Jem and Scout know if they are near the big oak
   tree?

    a. They can feel the wind getting warm.

    b. They can see the tree leaves falling.

    c. They can feel the ground getting cold.

    d. They can see the acorns scattered on the ground.

47) In Chapter 28, what happens to Bob Ewell?

    a. Bob Ewell gets fired.

    b. Bob Ewell is convicted.

    c. Bob Ewell moves away.

    d. Bob Ewell is found dead.

48) Among the following people, who is not involved in the fight on the
   night of the Halloween pageant?

    a. Heck Tate

b. Bob Ewell

c. Boo Radley

d. Jem Finch

49) In Chapter 29, when Scout first sees Boo Radley, where is he standing?

a. In front of his house

b. Inside Mr. Tate's car

c. In Jem's room

d. In Atticus's office

50) At the end of Chapter 30, which individual is Scout alluding to as a "mockingbird" in her statement, "It'd be sort of like shooting a mockingbird."?

a. Atticus Finch

b. Arthur Radley

c. Mayella Ewell

d. Jem Finch

▷ Sequencing Sentences

Arrange the following events in chronological order.

Part One

<Chapter 1 ~11>

1) Walter Cunningham is invited to dinner with the Finches.

2) Boo Radley comes out of his house and puts his blanket on Scout.

3) Dill comes to Maycomb to spend the summer with his aunt.

4) Scout finds two pieces of chewing gum in the knot-hole in the oak tree on the Radley Place.

5) Jem and Scout find the knot-hole filled with cement by Mr. Nathan Radley.

6) Atticus takes Jem and Scout to visit Aunt Alexandra to spend Christmas.

7) Jem loses his pants while running from the Radley Place with Scout and Dill after they hear the gunshot.

8) Atticus shoots a rabid dog in front of Jem and Scout.

9) Jem makes a snowman that resembles Mr. Avery out of dirt and covers it with snow.

10) Miss Maudie's house catches on fire and is burned down.

11) Jem ruins Mrs. Dubose's flower garden because she has been blaming

Atticus for defending black people.

Part Two

<Chapter 12 ~23>

1) Calpurnia takes Jem and Scout to her church, the First Purchase, and introduces them to her community.

2) Bob Ewell gives his testimony as a witness.

3) People in the black community bring food for Atticus to show their appreciation for defending Tom at the trial.

4) Tom gets convicted.

5) Scout finds Dill hiding under her bed.

6) Tom Robinson gives his testimony as a witness.

7) Mayella Ewell gives her testimony as a witness.

8) Mr. Dolphus Raymond tells Scout and Dill the truth about his pretending to be a drunk.

9) Atticus goes to the Maycomb jail to show the mob that he is determined to protect Tom Robinson.

10) Scout takes Dill outside the courtroom since Dill starts to cry.

<Chapter 24 ~31>

1) Arthur Radley asks Scout if she can take him home.

2) Atticus announces Tom's death.

3) Bob Ewell attacks Jem and Scout in the dark.

4) Bob Ewell is found dead under the tree where he attacked Jem and Scout.

5) Scout gets a role in the Halloween pageant.

6) Mr. Tate and Atticus agree that Bob Ewell was killed when he fell on his knife.

7) Mr. Tate figures out that Arthur Radley stabbed Bob Ewell to death while protecting Jem and Scout.

⟫⟫ Vocabulary Assessment

▷ Finding Synonyms

Connect each word with its synonym.

1) aberration   a. resolute; unyielding

2) acrimonious   b. anomaly; irregularity

3) adamant   c. aboriginal; endemic

4) connivance   d. judicious; careful

5) devout   e. bitter; acerbic

6) discreet   f. subdue; suppress

7) disposition   g. obstruction; hindrance

8) impediment   h. reticent; untalkative

9) indigenous   i. faithful; religious

10) mortification   j. conspiracy; collusion

11) quell   k. temperament; personality

12) taciturn   l. humiliation; embarrassment

▷ Finding Antonyms

Connect each word with its antonym.

1) acrimonious	a. nonnative; foreign
2) articulate	b. inarticulate; suppress
3) auspicious	c. kindhearted; gentle
4) cordial	d. inarticulate; ineloquent
5) disorderly	e. organized; systematic
6) enunciate	f. antagonistic; hostile
7) frivolous	g. consequential; important
8) illiterate	h. educated; intelligent
9) inconspicuous	i. discontinuous; ephemeral
10) indigenous	j. discouraging; hopeless
11) perpetual	k. noticeable; visible
12) prejudiced	l. disinterested; impartial

> Finding Definitions

Connect each word with its definition.

1) acquittal

2) antagonize

3) chronic

4) congregation

5) countenance

6) inequity

7) persecution

8) reminiscent

9) speculation

10) strenuous

11) uncompromising

12) vehement

a. cause to become hostile

b. showing aggressiveness

c. provoking a memory

d. requiring great exertion

e. discharge of an offense

f. constantly recurring

g. immoral behavior

h. conjecture without evidence

i. appearance of the face

j. not allowing for any exceptions

k. something that causes mental distress

l. assembled group for religious worship

》》 After-reading Activity

Crossword Puzzle

Solve the puzzle. You may find clues from the Vocabulary Assessment pages.

Word bank

Accost	Adjacent	Arbitrate	Assuage
Attentive	Bestow	Candid	Contradict
Demur	Dispel	Ensue	Façade
Indulge	Invoke	Prosecute	Reprimand
Rueful	Testify	Unanimous	Vapid
Venerable			

ACROSS

4. In agreement

6. Reach a settlement

8. Alleviate

9. Admonish

12. Respected

16. Exterior of a building

17. Satiate

18. Grant

19. Mournful

DOWN

1. Deny the truth of

2. Honest

3. Approach to speak

5. Bring action against

6. Concentrating

7. Drive away thought

10. Disagree

11. Give evidence

13. Nearby

14. Happen as a result

15. Lacking liveliness

17. Call upon

◆◆◆◆◆◆◆ To Kill a Mockingbird ◆◆◆◆◆◆◆

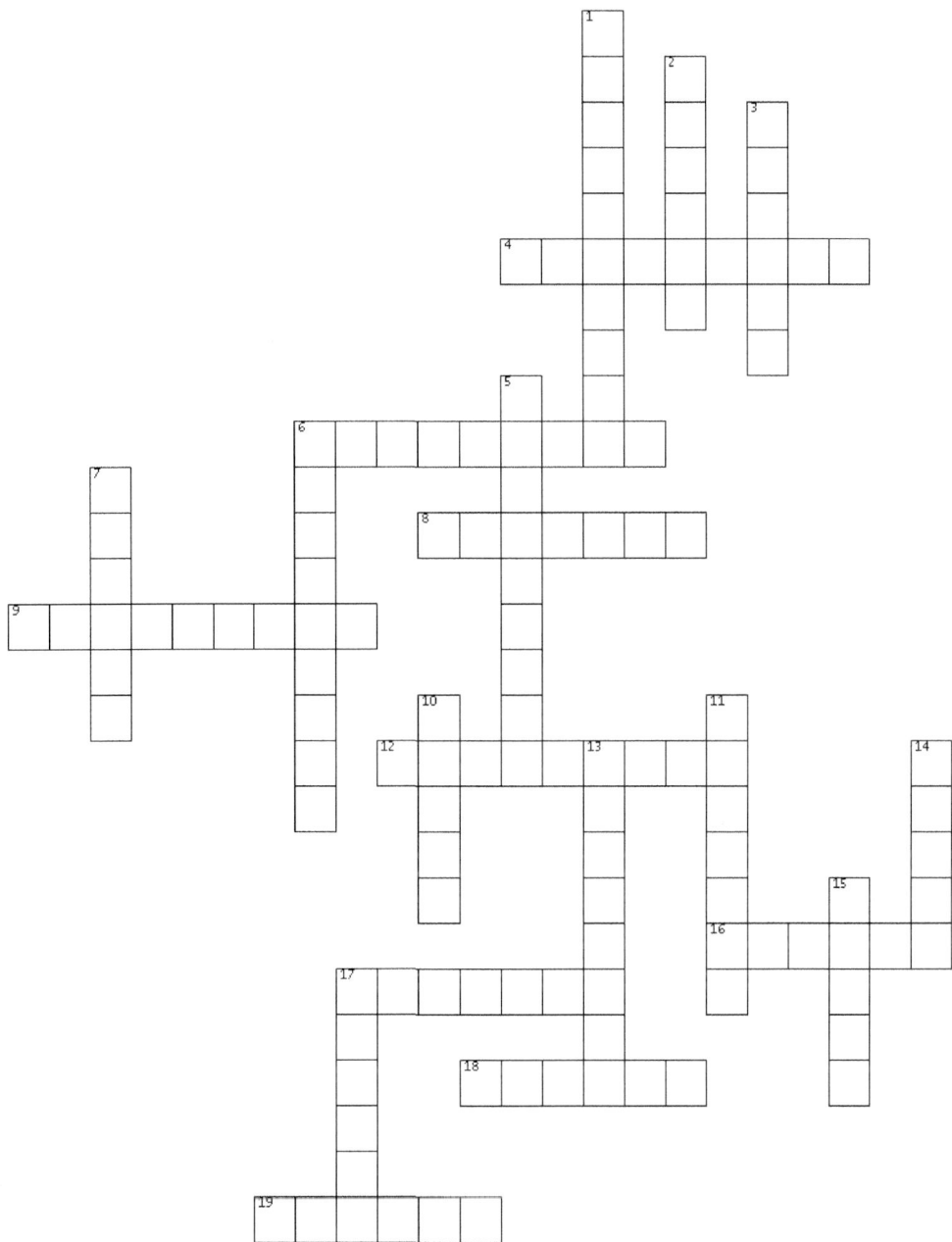

◆◆◆◆◆◆◆ Harper Lee ◆◆◆◆◆◆◆

Wordsearch

Find the characters' names in the puzzle. Words can go in any direction, and share letters as they cross over each other.

```
S  I  G  M  J  V  R  G  W  M  D  H  S  A  G
U  U  N  E  S  C  T  A  T  E  Q  W  U  R  I
U  I  C  J  W  T  A  H  D  Y  P  Y  Z  D  L
F  S  Y  I  A  A  I  L  C  L  S  I  O  N  M
E  U  Q  Y  T  Z  L  O  P  U  E  O  H  A  E
S  H  L  S  A  T  L  L  K  U  W  Y  X  X  R
R  O  O  S  B  V  A  E  E  R  R  T  X  E  F
R  A  R  U  H  T  R  A  E  Y  U  N  B  L  I
T  N  Y  E  K  O  I  D  C  O  A  B  I  A  N
B  M  L  M  V  M  N  J  C  Q  J  M  D  A  C
I  E  J  F  O  U  P  S  L  L  E  W  E  H  H
N  R  O  B  I  N  S  O  N  E  X  B  J  L  R
J  E  T  N  K  M  D  I  U  X  G  E  N  Q  Z
V  Y  T  W  H  B  N  P  W  Z  L  R  H  D  L
C  J  N  I  A  D  I  L  L  K  J  Q  S  C  Z
```

Alexandra	Dill	Helen	Tate
Arthur	Ewell	Jem	Taylor
Atticus	Finch	Mayella	Tom
Calpurnia	Gilmer	Radley	Underwood

≫ Answer Key

Pre-reading Discussion

Answers may vary.

Characters in the Story

n/a

Pre-reading Activity

Vocabulary List

n/a

Sentence Making

Answers may vary.

After-reading Discussion

Short Answer Questions

1) Calpurnia always wins because Atticus takes her side.

2) Making Boo Radley come out

3) Dill teases Jem for being scared of the Radley Place.

4) Miss Caroline is surprised and frustrated since Scout doesn't need to learn to read and write in Miss Caroline's teaching methods.

5) Walter Cunningham is too poor to bring lunch to school.

6) Answers may vary.

 Jem finds out that Walter Cunningham is one of his father's friends, Mr. Cunningham. / Walter must be hungry because he was not able to bring lunch that day.

7) Answers may vary.

Calpurnia wants to make up with Scout for what she has done to her that day. / Calpurnia has more free time than before since the children are at school.

8) Scout does not want to follow Miss Caroline's rules, which include not learning to read and write at home.

9) A compromise is an agreement reached by mutual concessions. Atticus and Scout compromise on the school policy that students should not learn to read and write at home.

10) Two pieces of chewing gum in wrappers

11) They can play with Dill in summer.

12) Good luck

13) They want to ask Boo Radley to come out to get some fresh air and have a chat with them.

14) Jem will be in trouble if Atticus learns about his attempt to make Boo Radley come out of his house.

15) Dill says he has won Jem's pants in a poker game.

16) Things they find are their properties if no one else claims the items for a couple of days.

17) They assume that the figurines are the carvings of Jem and Scout.

18) The knot-hole has been filled with cement.

19) Jem makes the snowman with dirt and covers it with snow. Atticus is impressed that Jem always has an idea.

20) Miss Maudie's house burns down.

21) Boo Radley puts his blanket on Scout's shoulders.

22) Atticus asks Scout to hold her head high and keep her fists down.

23) Aunt Alexandra thinks that it is inappropriate for Scout to wear overalls instead of dresses.

24) Scout thinks that Atticus looks old and cannot do anything that common people can do very well, except for just sitting and reading. However, Scout takes pride in Atticus when he shoots the rabid dog walking down the street in the distance with no mistake.

25) Jem gets furious at Mrs. Dubose for remarking Atticus as a person who is the same as the trash (black people) he works for.

26) Mrs. Dubose wants Jem to read to her every afternoon after school and Saturdays for two hours for a month.

27) Atticus is going to be absent on that Sunday, and Scout's church might not have a teacher.

28) A woman named Lula says that white children have their church and colored people have their own.

29) Maycomb people seldom marry people from outside. Many of them married into the same families.

30) Dill doesn't get enough attention from his mother and his stepfather at home.

31) Atticus is quietly reading, sitting on his office chair outside the jail while a mob is gathering.

32) If Calpurnia overhears their conversation, she may gossip on white people in her community.

33) Jem and Scout's presence made Mr. Cunningham view the situation from the perspective of Atticus, who is also a father just like him.

34) Answers may vary.

Atticus asks the question to show that Mr. Ewell doesn't care about his daughter's physical condition after the serious injuries. / If a doctor sees Mayella, he/she will find out that Mayella is not raped.

35) To show Judge Taylor that Mr. Ewell is left-handed

36) Tom Robinson may be left-handed, too.

37) Atticus is calling Mayella, "ma-am," and "Miss Mayella," which she has never been called as.

38) To show judge and the audience that Tom's left arm is seriously injured and unusable

39) Answers may vary.

Mayella doesn't have any friends. She cannot join black people's community nor join white people's community because she is not welcomed by either side.

40) Tom Robinson says that he feels sorry for Mayella since she seemed to be not getting any help from anybody in doing her chores.

41) Dill cannot stand the way Mr. Gilmer, the prosecutor, cross-examines Tom Robinson.

42) Mr. Link Deas abruptly adds his statement after Tom Robinson's testimony without an oath.

43) Even though Mr. Dolphus Raymond is known to be drinking alcohol in his disguised Coca-Cola sack, he drinks real cola most of the time, not alcohol. He is completely sober.

44) Aunt Alexandra sends Calpurnia to the courtroom to report to Atticus that Jem and Scout are missing.

45) Reverend Sykes has never seen any jury reach a verdict in favor of a colored man over a white man.

46) The black community brings Atticus all kinds of food to show him their respect on how he tried to defend Tom at the trial the previous day.

47) Answers may vary.

Miss Maudie says, "We're making a step."

48) A Cunningham, Walter Cunningham's double cousin, is hesitant about declaring a guilty verdict against Tom Robinson.

49) Atticus comes home early to accompany Calpurnia to Tom's house to tell Helen Robinson about her husband's death.

50) Dill says that Helen just fell down in the dirt like a giant stepped on her.

51) "One" means Tom Robinson, and "two" could be referring to Jem and Scout, since Mr. Ewell has a track record of victimizing those who are more powerless than him, such as his daughter and Tom Robinson.

52) Bob Ewell gets a job and gets fired in just a few days due to his laziness. Judge Taylor is injured by a burglar, presumably by Bob Ewell, while at home alone on a Sunday night. Helen Robinson, Tom's widow, is hired by Mr. Link Deas, the former employer of Tom.

53) Jem says that he keeps hearing some strange noise only when they are moving.

54) Scout's pink dress and her ham costume

55) Aunt Alexandra thinks she should have gone to the Halloween pageant and stayed with the kids.

56) The chicken wire of Scout's ham costume that circled around her

57) Scout realizes that Arthur has given Jem and Scout a lot of presents, but they never have given him anything back for what he has done for them.

58) Scout stands on the Radley porch, and recollects the events that have happened throughout the two years from Arthur's perspective.

In-Depth Writing Questions

1) Answers may vary.

Atticus is an exemplary father; he spends time with his children and answers their questions truthfully. He guides them to learn important values in life by setting an example for them, practicing those values himself. He places importance in making decisions based on conscientious and impartial judgment. He respects each of them as an independent person.

2) Answers may vary.

Miss Caroline fails to establish her authority in the classroom because she is insensitive to her students' needs, which is essential to building trust. For example, when she gives Walter Cunningham Jr. lunch money, she tells him to pay it back, leaving him feeling ashamed. On another occasion, she becomes greatly depressed when Burris Ewell leaves school on the first day of school. This indicates that she fails to understand the Ewell family's way of living. Lastly, she attempts to introduce her students to a new teaching method that is unfamiliar to them. Given these examples, it is only natural that the students do not want to place their trust in Miss Caroline.

3) Answers may vary.

Atticus says that Scout and her classmates should view things from Miss Caroline's perspective in order to understand her behavior. For example, when Miss Caroline gave Water Cunningham a quarter for his lunch, it must have been out of her generosity, not with the intention to offend him.

4) Answers may vary.

Scout wants to quit the game because she felt scared when she heard someone laughing from inside the Radley house as she rolled into the Radleys' front yard. Also, Atticus seemed to know that the kids have been playing the Boo Radley game.

5) Scout, Jem and Dill trespass into the backyard of the Radley house, and Mr. Nathan Radley shoots his gun in the air to warn the intruders.

Answers may vary. Example: While we were running away from the Radley house, Jem got stuck in the fence. As he kept running, he ended up leaving his pants on the fence. When Jem went back to retrieve his pants, they were neatly mended, and folded across the fence.

Jem is too stunned to tell Scout about the mended pants, so he takes some time to put the puzzle pieces together to understand the whole situation. Jem figures out that someone might have been watching their mischief and mended Jem's pants before Jem came to retrieve them.

6) Answers may vary.

I would describe Miss Maudie's reaction as resilient. After the fire, she says that she has always wanted a small house. She looks lively, and talks about Scout's unwitting encounter with Boo Radley the previous night rather than the fire. She is also more concerned about the commotion the fire caused to her neighborhood than about her burned-down house. She begins restoring her yard without asking others for help.

7) Miss Maudie says that Mockingbirds don't do any harm to us, but only sing for us. It is not right to bother people when they don't harm you, just living in their own way. In this context, "killing" means to pester Boo Radley to get out of his house when he doesn't want to.

8) Answers may vary.

Jem ruins Mrs. Dubose's flower garden to get revenge on her because she kept criticizing Atticus for defending black people. Although Mrs. Dubose has been badmouthing Atticus, it is reasonable for Jem to apologize to her because another person's ill-intended actions do not necessarily justify your own wrongdoings.

9) Answers may vary.

Based on the fact that Judge Taylor appointed Atticus to be Tom Robinson's lawyer, Atticus determines that the judge is trying his best to defend Tom. Atticus decides to take the case because he believes helping Tom Robinson is the right thing to do as a lawyer with conscience. He wants his kids to grow up making right choices as he does, so they won't regret having gone against their conscience in the future.

Answers may vary.

10) Atticus is satisfied with the way Calpurnia has brought up Jem and Scout, whereas Aunt Alexandra thinks Calpurnia, a black woman, is not appropriate for teaching the Finches' kids. Aunt Alexandra wants to make Calpurnia leave.

Jem tells Scout to not go against Aunt Alexandra because that may make their aunt confront Atticus, which would give Atticus a hard time when he already is getting stressed from Tom Robinson's impending trial.

11) Mr. Dolphus Raymond was supposed to marry a white lady, but she committed suicide when she found out that he had already been living with a black mistress, and had five kids with her. Even though he chooses to stay with the black community, he assumes that people will leave him alone if they think he is too drunk to make the right choices. Mr. Raymond prefers to associate with black people because he is more comfortable with people who don't care about his choices.

12) Tom Robinson is accused of raping and beating a white girl, Mayella Ewell. After Mr. Bob Ewell finds his daughter raped and cruelly beaten, he runs for Mr. Heck Tate to report the incident and ask him to be a witness, instead of calling a doctor to tend to his daughter's injury. This action is particularly incomprehensible because it is inconsistent with his statement that he cares about his daughter. Bob is also unable to elaborate on the reason why he didn't call a doctor.

Mayella is injured on her right side, and beaten around her right eye. These injuries are most likely to have been caused by a left-handed man, while Tom Robinson is right-handed.

13) Answers may vary.

Mr. Dolphus Raymond, who comes from a fine, wealthy family, chooses to associate with the black community since he lives with a black woman and had five children with her. He owns land and lives far away from the people in Maycomb. People are indifferent to him because they think he is a drunk person who lives quietly and independently. On the other hand, Mr. Bob Ewell, who is also from a white family, lives in the most squalid and dilapidated condition in Maycomb due to his ignorance, laziness, dishonesty, and filthiness. Bob Ewell is accepted by neither the white population nor the black not by his choice, but due to his meanness. While Mr. Raymond is confident with living in his own way of not bothering other people, Mr. Ewell harms other people for his convenience with no guilt, which leads him to be ostracized by the community.

14) Answers may vary.

As a colored man, Tom Robinson may have been worried that people could falsely accuse him of committing a crime, and if he were to get involved in such accusations, he would surely be prosecuted regardless of the truth.

Answers may vary.

15) Answers may vary.

The Jim Crow laws that legalized racial segregation in the Southern states of America severely damaged the social, economic, and political statuses of black people.

The Great Depression that took place from 1929 to 1939 had a widespread impact on all Americans. However, black people suffered more than any other racial group because they were the first to lose their jobs.

16) Mayella Ewell puts an innocent person's life at stake just to deny her own guilt of tempting a black man.

Bob Ewell savagely beats his own daughter and conspires with her to entrap Tom Robinson when he clearly knows that Tom will be convicted.

17) Bob and Mayella Ewell are confident that their lies won't be doubted, and the audience will agree with them under any circumstance since they are white. According to Atticus, their confidence is based on the wrong/evil assumption that all black people are immoral and, therefore, not to be trusted around white women.

18) Answers may vary.

19) Answers may vary.

For a case like Tom Robinson's, involving a white girl and a black man, it usually takes just a few minutes for the jury to reach a verdict, because a jury will always take the side that is favorable to the white person. Several hours of deliberation from the jury's part to give Tom a guilty verdict implied that they needed to take the time to consider the case more in-depth than usual, unable to quickly agree on the guilty verdict for the black man. This can be considered as the beginning of practicing impartial judgment in court, even if it still resulted in a guilty verdict for Tom.

20) Answers may vary.

Jem says that Scout shouldn't kill insects because they don't bother her. Later in this chapter, Mr. B.B. Underwood points out the resemblance of Tom's death to the senseless slaughter of songbirds by hunters. Both Scout's insect and Tom Robinson are mockingbirds that fall victim to the senseless act.

21) Answers may vary.

The Great Depression takes place in the United States in the 1930s, and at around the same time, the Jim Crow laws dominate the Southern United States, enforcing racial segregation. In Europe, The Nazi persecution of the Jews begins in 1933, annihilating a great number of the Jews. Miss Gates compares America and Germany to show the differences between democracy and dictatorship. She says that America is a democracy and Germany is a dictatorship.

She emphasizes that Americans are not prejudiced since they don't believe in persecuting anybody. Even though Miss Gates maintains that it is not right to persecute anybody, she fails to hide her animosity towards black people after Tom Robinson's trial, expressing that black people are not equal to the white, and need to learn a lesson from Tom Robinson's case.

22) Answers may vary.

Scout describes Arthur Radley as an innocuous, modest and unalarming man. She uses insipid colors to describe him: his hands are sickly white as if they have never seen the sun, his face is pale and hollow, and his eyes are colorless. However, in the beginning of the story, Boo Radley in Scout's imagination is viewed as unfriendly, mysterious, hermetic and savage. This impression changes as various events unfold, from hostile to hospitable.

23) Answers may vary.

When Scout first sees Arthur, she greets him, "Hey, Boo." She also calls him, "Come along, Mr. Arthur," when people go outside to her front porch, and takes him to the porch.

She offers Mr. Arthur a rocking-chair in a comparably dark spot considering that he may be more comfortable in the dark.

24) Answers may vary.

Upon hearing Scout's explanation, Atticus concludes that Jem killed Bob Ewell with Bob's knife. However, Mr. Tate confirms that Bob Ewell was killed by his own knife by mistake. Atticus cannot agree to Mr. Tate's statement because he doesn't want to let Jem think the truth can be tacitly covered. It is against his way of guiding his kids. However, when Mr. Tate says that it's a sin to take "him" into the light for what he has done for the town, Atticus realizes that Mr. Tate meant Boo Radley, and Boo Radley killed Bob while fighting him for the kids. Atticus is convinced to cover the truth to protect Boo Radley.

After-reading Assessment

Literary Analysis: Multiple-choice Questions

1) a	2) b	3) d	4) b	5) b
6) c	7) d	8) a	9) b	10) c
11) a	12) d	13) c	14) a	15) c
16) b	17) d	18) a	19) c	20) b
21) b	22) d	23) a	24) b	25) d
26) a	27) c	28) d	29) d	30) a
31) b	32) c	33) a	34) b	35) c
36) d	37) b	38) b	39) d	40) b

| 41) c | 42) b | 43) c | 44) a | 45) b |
| 46) c | 47) d | 48) a | 49) c | 50) b |

Sequencing Sentences

Part One

<Chapter 1~ Chapter 11>

3-1-4-7-5-9-10-2-6-8-11

Part Two

<Chapter 12~ Chapter 23>

1-5-9-2-7-6-10-8-4-3

<Chapter 24~ Chapter 31>

2-5-3-4-7-6-1

Vocabulary Assessment

Finding Synonyms

1) b

2) e

3) a

4) j

5) i

6) d

7) k

8) g

9) c

10) l

11) f

12) h

Finding Antonyms

1) c

2) d

3) j

4) f

5) e

6) b

7) g

8) h

9) k

10) a

11) i

12) l

Finding Definitions

1) e

2) a

3) f

4) l

5) i

6) g

7) k

8) c

9) h

10) d

11) j

12) b

After-reading Activity

Crossword Puzzle

ACROSS

4. Unanimous

6. Arbitrate

8. Assuage

9. Reprimand

12. Venerable

16. Façade

17. Indulge

18. Bestow

19. Rueful

DOWN

1. Contradict

2. Candid

3. Accost

5. Prosecute

6. Attentive

7. Dispel

10. Demur

11. Testify

13. Adjacent

14. Ensue

15. Vapid

17. Invoke

Harper Lee (April 28, 1926 ~ February 19, 2016)

Nelle Harper Lee was an American novelist best known for her novel *To Kill a Mockingbird* (1960). The book has become a classic of modern American literature, winning the 1961 Pulitzer Prize. For this novel, Harper Lee has also received numerous accolades and honorary degrees, including the Presidential Medal of Freedom in 2007.

The plot and characters of *To Kill a Mockingbird* are partly based on an event that occurred near her hometown, Monroeville, Alabama, in 1936. In *To Kill a Mockingbird*, the serious social and historical issues of rape and racial prejudice in the 1930s are depicted through the protagonist, Scout's eyes, in the first-person point of view. Through a series of events in the book, Harper Lee truthfully addresses issues of economic crisis during the Great Depression, different gender roles, social classes, and human conscience.

To Kill a Mockingbird was adapted into an Academy Award-winning film in 1962. The book has been translated into more than 40 languages, and sold more than 40 million copies worldwide.

Also available from Schoolhouse

ReCAP Workbooks

SCHOOLHOUSE — ReCAP Workbook — Freckle Juice

SCHOOLHOUSE — ReCAP Workbook — Charlotte's Web

SCHOOLHOUSE — ReCAP Workbook — Charlie and the Chocolate Factory

SCHOOLHOUSE — ReCAP Workbook — Because of Winn-Dixie

SCHOOLHOUSE — ReCAP Workbook — Matilda

SCHOOLHOUSE — ReCAP Workbook — HATCHET

SCHOOLHOUSE — ReCAP Workbook — Number the Stars

SCHOOLHOUSE — ReCAP Workbook — The Giver

SCHOOLHOUSE — ReCAP Workbook — Harry Potter and the Philosopher's Stone

SCHOOLHOUSE — ReCAP Workbook — To Kill a Mockingbird

Classic Stories Annotated for ReCAP

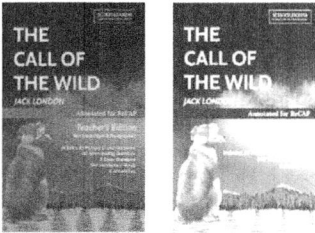

THE CALL OF THE WILD — JACK LONDON

THE CALL OF THE WILD — JACK LONDON

Classic Short Stories with Literary Analysis Questions

The Most Dangerous Game

The Last Leaf

The Gift of the Magi

The Necklace

O. Henry Short Stories: The Last Leaf & The Gift of the Magi

Aesop's Fables for Children — Annotated with Literary Analysis Questions

Printed in Great Britain
by Amazon